THE NAR

INSIDE THE MIND OF A NARCISSIST

Understanding the Complexities of

Narcissistic Personality Disorder

By: Kathlyn Jones

"Narcissism is the art of looking in the mirror

and seeing someone else." - Richard Stephenson

Chapter One:

Introduction to Narcissism:

Understanding the Personality Disorder

As I sat alone in my empty house, surrounded by the remnants of a life that once was, I couldn't help but wonder how it had all gone so wrong. How had the love between my spouse and I devolved into bitter resentment and animosity? It all started with a simple trait: narcissism.

At first, I was drawn to their confidence and charisma. They were the life of the party, and everyone gravitated towards them. But as time passed, I began to realize that their self-centeredness went beyond just being outgoing. They were obsessed with their appearance, constantly seeking validation from others and putting down anyone who didn't worship them.

Our marriage slowly but surely started to crumble under the weight of their narcissism. Every conversation became about them, and their needs and wants took priority over mine. They would belittle my accomplishments, gaslight me into thinking I was the problem, and refuse to take responsibility for their own mistakes.

As I tried to hold on to our relationship, I found myself losing pieces of myself in the process. I tried to be the perfect partner, constantly giving in to their demands and ignoring my own needs. But in the end, it was all for naught. Their constant need for attention and admiration left no room for anyone else, including me.

As I look back on our marriage, I realize that their narcissism was like cancer, slowly eating away at the foundation of our relationship until there was nothing left but bitterness and regret. It's a painful lesson to learn, but one that I hope others can avoid. Narcissism may seem appealing at first, but in the end, it will destroy everything in its path.

I used to be a confident person. I knew my worth, my skills, and my strengths. But as the years went by, being in a relationship with a narcissistic partner eroded my self-esteem until there was almost nothing left.

At first, I didn't realize what was happening. I thought I was being supportive, being a good partner by always putting their needs first. But as time passed, I started to feel more and more invisible. My opinions and feelings were dismissed, and any attempts I made to assert myself were met with anger and aggression.

It's hard to explain the slow, insidious way in which narcissism chips away at your self-worth. It's not always obvious or overt. It's the small comments that cut deep, the subtle put-downs that leave you questioning yourself, the constant invalidation that makes you doubt your own reality.

I remember feeling like I was constantly walking on eggshells, never knowing what might trigger an explosive reaction from my partner. I stopped speaking up for myself, stopped asserting my needs, stopped pursuing my own goals and dreams. I was so focused on trying to keep the peace and avoid conflict that I lost sight of who I was as a person.

It wasn't until I finally mustered the courage to leave the relationship that I realized just how much damage had been done. I had lost confidence in my abilities, my worth, and my identity. I felt like a shell of the person I used to be.

Rebuilding my self-worth has been a slow and painful process. It's taken therapy, support from friends and family, and a lot of self-reflection to start to regain some of what was lost. But even now, years later, there are still moments where I catch myself questioning my worth, second-guessing my decisions, and doubting my abilities.

Narcissism is a toxic and destructive force, and its effects can last long after the relationship has ended. It's a reminder to always prioritize your own needs, to trust your instincts, and to never allow anyone to make you feel small or insignificant.

Narcissism is a personality disorder characterized by an inflated sense of self-importance, an exaggerated need for admiration, and a lack of empathy for others. Individuals with a narcissistic personality disorder often have a sense of entitlement and believe they are superior to others. They tend to focus on their needs and desires and are often unable or unwilling to empathize.

If you are in a relationship with a narcissist, you may have experienced the harmful effects of their behavior. They may make you feel like you are walking on eggshells, constantly trying to avoid saying or doing something that will upset them. They may also belittle, criticize, or dismiss your feelings and needs.

Living with a narcissist can be an exhausting and emotionally draining experience. You may feel like you constantly give and never receive anything in return. You may also feel like you have lost yourself in the relationship, as the narcissist has a way of making everything about them.

It is essential to recognize the signs of narcissism and to seek help if you are in a relationship with a narcissist. Counseling can help you understand the relationship's dynamics and develop strategies for coping with the narcissist's behavior. Sometimes, it may be necessary to end the relationship to protect your well-being. Remember, you deserve to be treated with respect and kindness, and you do not have to tolerate abusive or unhealthy behavior from anyone.

Narcissism is a personality disorder characterized by a grandiose sense of self-importance, an excessive need for admiration, and a lack of empathy for others. Narcissistic individuals tend to exaggerate their achievements and abilities and may have an inflated sense of entitlement. While it is normal for people to have some degree of narcissism, it becomes problematic when it interferes with relationships and daily functioning.

One of the defining features of narcissism is the need for constant attention and admiration. Narcissistic individuals often go to great lengths to ensure they are the center of attention in any social situation. They may tell exaggerated stories about themselves, interrupt others, or engage in attention-seeking behaviors such as dressing provocatively or making grandiose gestures.

Another characteristic of narcissism is a lack of empathy for others. Narcissistic individuals tend to see other people as objects to be used for their benefit rather than as individuals with their thoughts and feelings. They may be highly manipulative and use others to achieve their goals without considering how their actions may affect others.

Narcissistic individuals often struggle with criticism and rejection, and they may become defensive or hostile when confronted with feedback that challenges their sense of self-worth. Similarly, they may quickly discard relationships or friendships that do not meet their high standards or threaten their sense of superiority.

In addition to their need for attention and admiration, narcissistic individuals often struggle with a sense of entitlement. They may believe they are entitled to special treatment or privileges simply because of who they are or what they have achieved. This entitlement can lead to frustration or anger when others disregard their needs or wants.

Narcissistic individuals may also engage in manipulative behaviors such as gaslighting, projection, and triangulation. Gaslighting involves manipulating someone into doubting their perception of reality, while projection involves projecting one's negative qualities onto others. Triangulation involves pitting two people against each other to control the situation.

Despite their many negative traits, narcissistic individuals may be able to develop healthier relationships and a greater sense of empathy with therapy and support. While holding them accountable for their actions and behaviors is essential, it is also important to recognize that narcissism is a complex disorder that can be challenging to treat.

One potential risk factor for the development of narcissism is childhood trauma. Children who experience neglect, abuse, or other forms of trauma may develop a sense of worthlessness or low self-esteem that can contribute to narcissism later in life. Similarly, children who are overvalued or praised excessively may also be at risk for developing narcissistic traits.

Narcissism is a complex personality disorder characterized by a grandiose sense of self-importance, a lack of empathy for others, and a need for attention and admiration. While narcissistic individuals can be challenging to interact with, they may be able to develop healthier relationships with therapy and support. Understanding the underlying causes and risk factors for narcissism can help us to better recognize and address this disorder in ourselves and others.

Chapter Two

The History of Narcissism: From Mythology to Modern Psychology

I had always known that my husband was a bit of a narcissist. He loved to talk about his accomplishments and put me down because he thought I didn't measure up to his standards.

But I never thought he would stoop to the level of narcissism against our children.

It started with little comments and jokes that were meant to be harmless but left me feeling uncomfortable. I first brushed them off, thinking I was being too sensitive. But then the comments became more frequent and aggressive against our daughters.

My husband would criticize my daughter's appearance, telling them they needed to dress more femininely to get ahead. He would make inappropriate comments about women and their worth, telling our daughters that a woman's place was in the home to cook, clean, and care for her family. And when I tried to stand up for my daughters, he would brush me off or turn the tables on me, making me feel like I was the one in the wrong.

It was a toxic and demoralizing environment, but I felt trapped. I didn't have a job and didn't want to be seen as weak or unable to handle the pressure. So I kept my head down and tried to ignore the constant barrage of insults and harassment.

It wasn't until my daughters started exhibiting mental fatigue that I realized how toxic the environment had become. I knew then that I had to get out of there because my self-esteem and my daughter's self-esteem started becoming increasingly demoralized. I knew I had to do something to stop the cycle.

Narcissism has been a part of human psychology since recorded history began. From ancient Greek mythology to modern-day social media influencers, excessive self-love and admiration have taken many forms over the centuries. But where did this idea of narcissism come from, and how has it evolved? How did my husband, who didn't smoke, drink, take drugs, or cheat, become such a toxic and unbearable man?

The concept of narcissism has its roots in Greek mythology. Narcissus was a handsome hunter who was known for his beauty and arrogance. One day, while hunting in the woods, he saw his reflection in a pond and fell in love with it. He was so enamored with his image that he refused to leave the pond and eventually died there, consumed by his vanity.

The term "narcissism" was first used in modern psychology by Sigmund Freud in the early 20th century. Freud believed that narcissism was a normal part of human development, particularly in the early stages of life. He suggested that infants and young children were naturally self-centered and necessary for their growth and development.

However, Freud also recognized that some people could become fixated on their own selves and develop an excessive and unhealthy level of self-love. He referred to this as "pathological narcissism" and suggested that it was a disorder that could have serious negative consequences for individuals and society.

Since Freud's time, researchers and psychologists have continued to study narcissism and its effects on individuals and society. They have identified different types of narcissism, such as grandiose narcissism (characterized by a sense of superiority and entitlement) and vulnerable narcissism (marked by a need for admiration and attention).

Some researchers have also suggested that cultural and societal factors may contribute to the development of narcissism. For example, some have argued that modern society's emphasis on individualism and self-promotion may encourage narcissistic tendencies in some individuals.

In recent years, the study of narcissism has become increasingly important in politics, business, and social media. Some researchers have suggested that narcissistic individuals may be more likely to seek positions of power and influence, which could negatively affect society.

Others have suggested that the proliferation of social media and the internet may contribute to expanding narcissistic tendencies. Notably, social media platforms facilitate enhancing and promoting one's image and easily acquiring recognition and approval.

Regardless of the growing interest in narcissism, researchers still do not know much about the disorder. For example, it is unclear why some individuals develop narcissistic tendencies while others do not, and there is debate about the best approaches for treating narcissistic personality disorder.

Despite these challenges, the study of narcissism remains an important area of research in psychology and related fields. By continuing to explore the history and development of narcissism, researchers may better understand this complex and often difficult-to-treat disorder and develop more effective interventions for those who struggle with it.

Chapter Three:
The Different Types of Narcissism:
Identifying the Variations

It's easy to think of narcissism as a purely negative trait, something that only exists in the minds of cruel and selfish people. But the truth is that many good and well-meaning individuals like my husband can also be destroyed by their narcissistic tendencies. It's a paradoxical and complex phenomenon, one that requires a nuanced understanding of the human psyche and the role that ego plays in our lives.

At its core, narcissism is a form of self-love, a desire to be seen and appreciated for our unique qualities and accomplishments. This isn't inherently bad, and in fact, a healthy sense of self-esteem and self-worth can be a powerful tool for achieving our goals and living a fulfilling life.

However, when this desire for recognition and admiration becomes excessive and all-consuming, it can lead to destructive behaviors and thought patterns. People who struggle with narcissism may become obsessed with their own success and achievements, to the point where they are willing to sacrifice the well-being of others in order to maintain their status and reputation.

For my husband, this meant engaging in unethical or immoral behavior, lying or cheating to get ahead, or exploiting his family for personal gain. For others, it may mean becoming so consumed with their own self-image that they neglect the needs and feelings of those around them, causing pain and damage to their relationships and friendships.

In either case, the end result for my husband was a profound sense of loneliness and isolation, as his ego-driven actions pushed away those who deeply cared for him. He eventually became trapped in a cycle of self-obsession, unable to break free from his own destructive tendencies.

It wasn't an easy realization to come to, but after years of feeling unseen, unheard, and emotionally drained, I finally recognized that my husband was a narcissist. At first, I didn't want to believe it. I made excuses for his behavior, telling myself that he was just under a lot of stress or that he didn't mean to hurt me. But as time went on, I couldn't ignore the constant gaslighting, manipulation, and belittling that had become a part of our daily interactions. It wasn't until I started reading about the signs and symptoms of narcissism that I began to see our relationship for what it truly was - a toxic and one-sided dynamic that was slowly chipping away at my self-worth and happiness. Once I had the language and the tools to recognize his behavior for what it was, I was able to start taking steps towards healing and ultimately, breaking free from the cycle of abuse.

However, it was not easy to understand the issue because narcissism is a complex and multifaceted personality trait, one that can take many different forms and manifest in a wide variety of behaviors. From grandiose and overtly self-absorbed individuals to those who hide their narcissism behind a mask of humility and selflessness, there are countless ways in which this trait can present itself. Identifying the different kinds of selfishness can help understand the disorder and develop practical treatment approaches. Here are some of the most commonly recognized types of narcissism:

Grandiose Narcissism - A sense of superiority, entitlement, and grandiosity characterizes this type of narcissism. Individuals with grandiose narcissism may believe they are better than others and may have an inflated sense of their importance and achievements.

Vulnerable Narcissism - Vulnerable narcissism is characterized by a need for admiration and attention and a fear of rejection and criticism. Individuals with vulnerable narcissism may be more sensitive to criticism and may struggle with low self-esteem.

Malignant Narcissism - Malignant narcissism is a particularly severe and dangerous form of narcissism characterized by a combination of grandiosity, aggression, and sadism. Individuals with malignant narcissism may exploit and manipulate others for their own gain.

Covert Narcissism – Covert narcissism is characterized by a more subtle and understated form. Individuals with covert narcissism may appear humble and self-effacing but may have a strong sense of entitlement and a need for admiration.

Communal Narcissism – Communal narcissism is a type of narcissism that is focused on the collective rather than the individual. Individuals with communal narcissism may believe their group or community is superior to others and may feel a strong loyalty and commitment to their group.

Somatic Narcissism – Somatic narcissism is characterized by a preoccupation with physical appearance and attractiveness. Individuals with somatic narcissism may spend excessive amounts of time and money on their appearance and may be particularly sensitive to criticism or perceived flaws.

Cerebral Narcissism - Cerebral narcissism is characterized by a focus on intellectual ability and achievement. Individuals with cerebral narcissism may be knowledgeable and may have a strong need to demonstrate their intellectual superiority to others.

Identifying the different types of narcissism can be a helpful first step in developing practical treatment approaches. Depending on the type of narcissism and its severity, treatment may involve a combination of therapy, medication, and lifestyle changes. By tailoring treatment to the individual's specific needs and characteristics, it may be possible to help them overcome their narcissistic tendencies and lead a more fulfilling life.

Chapter Four

The Development of Narcissism: Causes and Contributing Factors

I never imagined that the man I married would be the one to hurt me the most, but my husband's narcissism hurt me in ways I never thought possible. At first, it was subtle - a comment here, a dismissive gesture there. But over time, his behavior became more overt, and I found myself walking on eggshells around him, never sure what might set him off or trigger an outburst. He belittled me, criticized me, and made me feel like I was never good enough. I stopped expressing my opinions, stopped pursuing my own interests, stopped being myself in order to avoid his wrath.

His need for control and admiration extended to all aspects of our life together. He controlled the finances, the social calendar, even the decor of our home. I became isolated from my friends and family, as he convinced me that they didn't understand us or that they were somehow a threat to our relationship. His constant need for attention and validation left me feeling neglected and unimportant, like I was nothing more than an accessory to his perfect life.

It took me a long time to recognize the damage that his behavior was causing me. I lost my sense of self-worth, my self-esteem, and my confidence. I became depressed, anxious, and constantly on edge, never knowing when he might lash out or demand more of me. It was only after seeking help and support that I was able to start rebuilding my life, reclaiming my independence, and healing from the trauma that his narcissism had inflicted upon me.

My husband was not a physically abusive man, but he suffered from a range of different factors that influenced his narcissistic complex.

Here are some of the most commonly recognized causes and contributing factors of narcissism:

Genetics – Studies have suggested that narcissism may have a genetic component. Some research has found that narcissistic traits may be inherited, and individuals with a family history of narcissism may be more likely to develop the disorder.

Childhood experiences – Childhood experiences can play a significant role in the development of narcissism. Some researchers believe that early childhood experiences of neglect, abuse, or trauma can lead to developing narcissistic tendencies to cope with emotional pain and insecurity.

Parental overvaluation – Many researchers have suggested that parental overvaluation may contribute to the development of narcissism. This occurs when parents excessively praise and overvalue their child, leading the child to develop an exaggerated sense of self-importance and entitlement.

Cultural and societal factors - According to some studies, the development of narcissism may be influenced by cultural and socioeconomic variables. Others have claimed, for instance, that contemporary society's focus on individuality and self-promotion may foster narcissistic tendencies in some people.

Adverse life events - Adverse life events such as loss, trauma, or rejection may contribute to developing narcissistic tendencies. Some individuals may use narcissistic traits as a coping mechanism to protect themselves from further emotional pain or rejection.

Insecure attachment - Insecure attachment styles, such as anxious or avoidant attachment, have been identified as potential contributing factors to the development of narcissism. Individuals with insecure attachment styles may struggle with feelings of insecurity and a need for validation and attention.

Personality traits - Certain personality traits, such as low empathy or high neuroticism, have been linked to the development of narcissism. Individuals with these traits may be more prone to developing narcissistic tendencies as a way of coping with emotional distress or feelings of inadequacy.

Chapter Five:

The Narcissistic Personality: Traits and Characteristics

When I first met my husband, I was drawn to his charm, confidence, and magnetic personality. But as our relationship progressed, I began to see a darker side of him - one that was marked by selfishness, manipulation, and a constant need for admiration and attention.

As I learned more about narcissistic personality disorder, I started to recognize the traits in my husband's behavior. He was grandiose, always talking about his accomplishments and insisting that he was the best at everything he did. He lacked empathy, unable to truly connect with me on an emotional level or understand the impact that his words and actions had on me.

He was also highly manipulative, using guilt, fear, and shame to control my behavior and keep me isolated from my friends and family. He demanded constant admiration and validation, always seeking out praise and attention from those around him.

Over time, his narcissistic traits became more pronounced and destructive, causing me immense pain and suffering. But it wasn't until I began to educate myself about the disorder that I was able to see our relationship for what it truly was – a poisonous and one-sided relationship that was progressively eroding my self-worth and happiness.

Narcissistic Personality Disorder (NPD) is a mental disorder characterized by self-importance, a desire for praise, and a lack of empathy for others. People with this personality disorder often overstate their accomplishments and abilities and need continual external affirmation. Those with a narcissistic personality disorder may also feel entitlement and expect others to meet their needs, resulting in problematic relationships and interactions with others.

Narcissistic persons often exhibit an inflated sense of self-worth and a superiority complex. To maintain their inflated self-worth, they may overstate their successes and talents and seek praise and admiration from others. This may result in a lack of care for others and an emphasis on self-promotion, which can harm relationships and cause difficulties in the workplace or in social circumstances.

Another key trait of NPD is a lack of empathy and a disregard for others' feelings and needs. Narcissistic individuals may have difficulty understanding or caring about the emotional states of others and may only be able to see them as extensions of themselves rather than as separate individuals with their own needs and feelings. This can lead to a lack of consideration for others and a tendency to manipulate or exploit them for their own gain.

In addition to their lack of empathy, narcissistic individuals may also have difficulty regulating their own emotions. They may be prone to sudden outbursts of anger or frustration when their grandiose sense of self-worth is threatened and may be hypersensitive to criticism or rejection. This can lead to erratic and unpredictable behavior and difficulty maintaining stable relationships.

Narcissistic individuals may also feel entitled, believing they deserve special treatment or privileges due to their perceived superiority. They may become upset or angry if they feel that others are not treating them as they believe they should be treated and may expect others to cater to their every whim. This can create problems in social and work situations and lead to a lack of personal growth and development.

Narcissistic personalities may also struggle with intimacy and close relationships. Their focus on themselves and their own needs can make it difficult for them to form meaningful connections with others, and they may struggle to empathize with or understand their partner's perspective. This can lead to a pattern of shallow, short-lived relationships and a lack of intimacy or emotional depth in their interactions with others.

The traits and characteristics of the narcissistic personality can create significant difficulties in social, personal, and work situations. While some individuals with NPD may seek treatment and make progress toward greater empathy and self-awareness, others may continue to struggle with their grandiose sense of self-worth and lack of empathy for others.

Chapter Six:

The Impact of Narcissism: How it Affects Relationships and Society

My husband's narcissism had a profound impact on our marriage, turning what should have been a loving and supportive partnership into a one-sided dynamic that left me feeling isolated, unsupported, and unimportant. I truly loved my husband, but despite my efforts to salvage our relationship, his narcissistic behavior continued to erode our marriage until it was nothing more than a shell of what it once was. Ultimately, I had to make the difficult decision to leave, in order to protect my own well-being and begin the process of healing and rebuilding my life.

The influence of narcissism on relationships and society may be substantial. People with narcissistic tendencies often put their wants and interests ahead of those of others, resulting in difficulties in their personal and professional relationships. These people may also pursue positions of power and influence, which may have far-reaching social consequences.

In personal relationships, narcissistic individuals may struggle to form and maintain meaningful connections with others. Their focus on themselves and their own needs can make it difficult for them to empathize with their partner and understand their perspective. Narcissistic individuals may also struggle with intimacy and emotional depth, leading to a pattern of shallow, short-lived relationships.

Narcissistic tendencies can also have a significant impact on professional relationships. Individuals with narcissistic tendencies may prioritize their own success and achievements over those of their colleagues, leading to a competitive and cutthroat work environment. They may also struggle to work collaboratively with others, preferring to work alone or take credit for the work of others.

In broader society, narcissistic individuals may seek out positions of power and influence. They may be drawn to political, business, or entertainment careers, where fame and public recognition can reinforce their grandiose sense of self-worth. This can lead to problems in governance and leadership, as narcissistic individuals may prioritize their own interests and desires above those of their constituents or employees.

Narcissistic individuals may also struggle to understand or care about the needs and perspectives of marginalized or vulnerable populations. Their lack of empathy and focus on their needs can lead to policies and actions that harm these populations, further exacerbating social inequalities and injustices.

In addition to its impact on personal and professional relationships, narcissism can also have a broader impact on societal norms and values. The emphasis on individual success and achievement over community and collaboration can lead to a culture of hyper-competitiveness and self-promotion. This can make it difficult for individuals to prioritize the broader community's needs and work towards collective goals.

Overall, the impact of narcissism can be significant and far-reaching. While some individuals with narcissistic tendencies may seek treatment and make progress toward greater empathy and self-awareness, others may continue to prioritize their own needs and desires at the expense of their relationships and society as a whole.

Chapter Seven:

The Narcissistic Family: Patterns and Dynamics

When I first met my husband's family, I was struck by their charm, confidence, and magnetic personalities. They seemed to have it all - successful careers, beautiful homes, and a seemingly perfect family dynamic. But as I spent more time with them, I began to see a darker side of their behavior - one that was marked by selfishness, manipulation, and a constant need for admiration and attention.

It soon became clear that my husband's family had a long history of narcissistic behavior. From his parents to his siblings, they all exhibited the same traits - a lack of empathy, an obsession with appearance and status, and a deep-seated need for control and admiration.

As I learned more about narcissism and its impact on families, I started to see how my husband's upbringing had affected him. His parents had always placed a premium on success and achievement, pushing him to excel academically and professionally at all costs. They would criticize him harshly for any perceived failures, leaving him with a deep-seated sense of inadequacy and a constant need to prove himself.

His siblings were no better, constantly vying for attention and validation from their parents and each other. They would belittle my husband and each other, always trying to one-up each other with their achievements or accomplishments.

Despite the toll that his family's narcissism had taken on him, my husband had always seemed resilient and determined to break the cycle. But as our relationship progressed, I began to see how deeply ingrained his narcissistic behavior was, and how much work it would take for him to overcome The Narcissistic Family Trait.

The Narcissistic Family is a term used to describe a family system where one or more members exhibit narcissistic personality traits. In these families, the focus is often on the needs and desires of the narcissistic member, leading to a breakdown in communication, emotional intimacy, and healthy relationships. Here are some patterns and dynamics that are common in the Narcissistic Family.

1. The Narcissistic Family often revolves around the needs of the narcissistic member. This

individual may demand attention, validation, and admiration from other family members and become angry or manipulative if these needs are unmet. This can create an environment where other family members feel they must constantly cater to the narcissistic member's desires at the expense of their own needs and desires.

2. Communication in the Narcissistic Family is often fraught with tension and miscommunication. The narcissistic member may struggle to understand or care about the emotional states of others, leading to a lack of empathy and emotional intimacy within the family. Other family members may become resentful or angry at the narcissistic member's behavior, leading to conflict and further breakdown in communication.

3. Boundaries in the Narcissistic Family may be blurred or nonexistent. The narcissistic member may feel entitled to invade other family

members' personal space or boundaries, leading to discomfort and violation. Other family members may also struggle to establish and maintain their own boundaries, leading to a lack of autonomy and agency within the family system.

4. The Narcissistic Family may struggle with emotional neglect or abuse. The narcissistic member's focus on their own needs and desires may lead to a lack of emotional support and validation for other family members. Additionally, the narcissistic member may become angry or abusive if their needs are not met, leading to a toxic and offensive environment within the family.

5. Scapegoating is a familiar dynamic in the Narcissistic Family. One or more family members may be singled out as the cause of the family's problems, even though the issues may be rooted in the narcissistic member's behavior.

The scapegoated member may be blamed for everything that goes wrong in the family, leading to feelings of guilt, shame, and isolation.

6. The Narcissistic Family may struggle with enmeshment or codependency. Family members may become overly dependent on the narcissistic member for emotional support and validation, leading to a lack of independence and autonomy. This can also create a dynamic where the narcissistic member feels entitled to control or manipulate the actions and emotions of other family members.

7. The Narcissistic Family may prioritize image and appearance over emotional health and well-being. The family may go to great lengths to maintain a façade of perfection and success, despite the family's underlying dysfunction and emotional turmoil. This can lead to feelings of isolation and shame for family members, who

may feel they cannot speak out about the problems in the family.

8. The Narcissistic Family may struggle with generational patterns of narcissism. Children of narcissistic parents may develop their narcissistic tendencies, either as a way of coping with the dysfunction within the family or as a learned behavior. This can perpetuate the cycle of narcissism and dysfunction within the family system.

A breakdown in healthy communication, emotional intimacy, and boundaries characterizes the Narcissistic Family. The focus on the needs and desires of the narcissistic member can lead to emotional neglect or abuse, scapegoating, enmeshment, and generational patterns of dysfunction. Therapy can help family members to recognize and address these patterns, establish healthy boundaries, and work towards more excellent emotional health and well-being.

Chapter Eight:

The Narcissistic Workplace: Recognizing and Coping with Narcissistic Colleagues

Being a business owner requires a certain level of confidence, assertiveness, and drive. But when those qualities are coupled with narcissistic behavior, the results can be disastrous.

As the spouse of a business owner who is also a narcissist, I've seen firsthand how his need for control and admiration can permeate every aspect of his professional life. He's always looking for ways to prove his superiority, whether it's through financial success, industry accolades, or social status.

But his narcissism also manifests in more insidious ways. He's highly critical of his employees and colleagues, rarely giving credit where it's due and always taking the lion's share of the credit for any successes. He's quick to anger if things don't go his way, often lashing out at those around him and creating a toxic work environment.

Despite the toll that his behavior takes on those around him, my husband is unable to see the damage he's causing. He's convinced that he's the only one who can truly lead his company to success, and he refuses to take feedback or criticism from anyone else.

As his spouse, I've struggled to balance my support for his professional aspirations with the knowledge that his narcissism is causing real harm to those around him. I've watched as employees quit or are fired, unable to withstand the pressure of working for a boss who demands absolute obedience and adoration.

Ultimately, I've had to come to terms with the fact that my husband's narcissism isn't just a personal issue - it's a professional one as well. And as much as I love and support him, I know that he'll never be able to fully succeed until he's able to confront and overcome his own Narcissistic Workplace Tendencies.

The Narcissistic Workplace is a term used to describe a work environment where one or more colleagues exhibit narcissistic personality traits. These individuals may prioritize their own needs and desires over the needs of the team or organization, leading to a breakdown in communication, teamwork, and productivity. Here are some tips for recognizing and coping with narcissistic colleagues in the workplace.

It is important to recognize the signs of narcissistic behavior. Narcissistic individuals may exhibit a sense of entitlement, a lack of empathy, and a need for admiration and validation. They may also be manipulative, controlling, and unwilling to take responsibility for their mistakes or shortcomings. Recognizing these signs can help you to understand the dynamics at play in your workplace and to develop strategies for coping with these individuals.

It is essential to maintain healthy boundaries with narcissistic colleagues. This may involve setting clear expectations for communication and behavior and refusing to use manipulative or controlling tactics. It may also include limiting your interactions with the narcissistic colleague, where possible, and avoiding getting caught up in their drama or emotional turmoil.

It is important to stay focused on your own goals and objectives in the workplace. Narcissistic colleagues may undermine your confidence or diminish your accomplishments to bolster your sense of superiority. By staying focused on your work and achievements, you can maintain a sense of purpose and motivation and avoid getting drawn into power struggles or competition with your narcissistic colleague.

It is crucial to building a support network within the workplace. This may involve cultivating positive relationships with colleagues or seeking a mentor or trusted advisor who can provide guidance and support. By building a strong network of allies and supporters, you can mitigate the impact of the narcissistic colleague on your work and emotional well-being.

It is important to communicate assertively and effectively with narcissistic colleagues. This may involve using "I" statements to express your feelings and concerns rather than attacking or blaming the other person. It may also include setting clear boundaries around communication and behavior and being willing to walk away from a conversation or interaction if it becomes abusive or manipulative.

It is important to practice self-care and stress management techniques in the workplace. Dealing with a narcissistic colleague can be emotionally draining and stressful, and taking steps to maintain your own well-being is essential. This may involve practicing mindfulness, exercise, or other stress-reducing techniques, taking breaks when needed, and seeking support from friends and family outside of work.

It is crucial that you document any incidents of abusive or manipulative behavior by the narcissistic colleague. This may be helpful if you need to escalate the situation to a manager or HR representative or if you need to protect yourself from potential retaliation or defamation.

It is important to seek professional support if you are experiencing ongoing emotional distress or anxiety due to your interactions with a narcissistic colleague. A therapist or counselor can provide guidance and support in coping with the emotional impact of workplace dynamics and help you develop strategies for managing stress and maintaining your emotional well-being.

Lastly, it is important to recognize that you may not be able to change the behavior of a narcissistic colleague. Sometimes, the best strategy may be to disengage from the relationship as much as possible and focus on your work and well-being. By recognizing the limitations of your control over the situation, you can avoid getting caught up in power struggles or attempts to change the other person and focus on what is within your power to control.

Chapter Nine:

Narcissism and Mental Health:

Comorbidities and Treatment Options

When I first learned about my husband's narcissistic behavior, I held out hope that he would be able to overcome it on his own. I believed that with enough love and support, he could change his ways and become the caring, empathetic partner that I had always hoped for.

But as time went on, it became clear that my husband's narcissism was deeply ingrained and unlikely to change without professional help. His need for control and admiration, coupled with his inability to empathize with those around him, had caused significant damage to our relationship.

I urged him to seek therapy, to work with a professional who could help him confront and overcome his narcissistic tendencies. But he was resistant, insisting that there was nothing wrong with him and that any problems in our relationship were my fault.

I watched helplessly as his behavior continued to worsen, causing increasing strain on our marriage. He would lash out at me over minor disagreements, demanding that I validate his feelings and opinions at all times. He would refuse to listen to my perspective or acknowledge my needs, dismissing them as irrelevant or unimportant.

Despite my efforts to encourage him to seek treatment, my husband remained steadfast in his denial of any problems. I found myself growing resentful and frustrated, realizing that I couldn't fix him or make him change.

Looking back, I wish that my husband had been willing to confront his narcissism and seek professional help. Maybe then, we could have salvaged our relationship and built a healthier, happier future together. But as it stands, his unwillingness to acknowledge his behavior and seek treatment for his mental health issues was a significant factor in the demise of our marriage.

Narcissism is a personality disorder that can lead to significant mental health problems for individuals and those around them. A narcissistic personality disorder is often comorbid with other mental health conditions such as depression, anxiety, and substance abuse. Treatment options for narcissism and its comorbidities may involve a combination of psychotherapy and medication.

Individuals with a narcissistic personality disorder may also struggle with depression, anxiety, and substance abuse. Depression and anxiety can be caused by the individual's need for admiration and validation and their tendency to view themselves as superior to others. Substance abuse may be a way for the individual to cope with feelings of inadequacy or to numb their emotional pain.

Treatment options for narcissism and its comorbidities may involve a combination of psychotherapy and medication. Psychotherapy may include cognitive-behavioral therapy, interpersonal therapy, or psychoanalytic therapy. These therapies aim to help the individual understand their behavior and thought patterns and develop healthier coping mechanisms and interpersonal skills.

Medication may be used to treat comorbid conditions such as depression, anxiety, or substance abuse. Antidepressants, anti-anxiety medications, and medications for addiction may be prescribed to help the individual manage their symptoms and improve their mental health. However, medication alone is unlikely to be effective in treating narcissistic personality disorder.

It is also essential for individuals with a narcissistic personality disorder to engage in self-care and stress management techniques. This may include exercise, mindfulness, and other stress-reducing activities. Individuals with narcissistic personality disorder can reduce their symptoms and improve their overall mental health by focusing on their well-being and emotional regulation.

Family therapy may also be an effective treatment option for individuals with a narcissistic personality disorder. Family therapy can help the individual and their loved ones understand the behavior and communication patterns contributing to the condition. By working together to develop healthier communication and interpersonal skills, the family can create a more supportive and nurturing environment for the individual with a narcissistic personality disorder.

It is important to note that treatment for narcissism and its comorbidities can be challenging. Success may depend on the individual's willingness to engage in treatment and change their behavior and thought patterns. Individuals with a narcissistic personality disorder may resist treatment, as they may not see their behavior as problematic or may be unwilling to take responsibility for their actions.

Individuals with a narcissistic personality disorder may sometimes benefit from group therapy or support groups. These groups can provide a safe and supportive environment for individuals with similar experiences to share their stories and offer each other support and encouragement.

Ultimately, treatment for narcissism and its comorbidities requires a holistic approach that considers the individual's unique needs and circumstances. Individuals with narcissistic personality disorder can improve their mental health and overall well-being by working with a mental health professional and engaging in self-care and stress management techniques.

Chapter Ten:

Healing from Narcissistic Abuse: Recovery and Moving Forward

Healing from the emotional wounds inflicted by a narcissistic partner can be a long and difficult journey. As someone who has been through this process, I know firsthand how overwhelming it can feel to try and move forward after being married to a narcissist.

The first step in my healing journey was acknowledging the reality of my situation. I had to accept that my ex-husband's behavior was not my fault, and that I couldn't fix or change him. This was a painful realization, but it was also liberating - it allowed me to let go of the guilt and self-blame that had been weighing me down for so long.

From there, I focused on taking care of myself. I sought out therapy and support groups, talking through my experiences with others who had been through similar situations. I learned how to set healthy boundaries and prioritize my own needs, rather than always putting my ex-husband's needs first.

It was a slow process, but over time, I started to feel more empowered and in control of my life. I found new hobbies and activities that brought me joy, and I started to rebuild my social support network.

But perhaps the most important aspect of my healing journey was learning to trust myself again. Narcissistic partners often undermine their victim's sense of self-worth and agency, leaving them feeling lost and powerless. By reconnecting with my own intuition and inner wisdom, I was able to rediscover my own strength and resilience.

It hasn't always been easy, but I'm proud of the progress I've made in my healing journey. While the wounds inflicted by a narcissistic partner can run deep, it's possible to heal and rebuild a happier, healthier life on the other side.

Healing from narcissistic abuse can be difficult and complex, but it is possible with time, effort, and support. Narcissistic abuse can leave deep emotional wounds that may take time to heal, but there are several steps that individuals can take to begin the process of recovery and move forward with their lives.

The first step in healing from narcissistic abuse is to acknowledge that the abuse has occurred and recognize its impact on your life. This can involve accepting that the person who is supposed to love and care for you has been manipulative, controlling, and abusive.

The next step is to seek support. This can include talking to friends, family, or a therapist who can provide validation, empathy, and guidance. Support groups for survivors of narcissistic abuse can also be a valuable resource for individuals who may feel isolated or alone in their experiences.

Another essential step in healing from narcissistic abuse is to establish boundaries. This can involve limiting contact with the abuser, identifying and avoiding triggers, and learning to say no to unreasonable demands. Establishing limitations can help individuals regain control over their lives and reduce their vulnerability to further abuse.

Self-care is also an essential part of the healing process. This may involve engaging in activities that bring joy and pleasure, such as exercise, hobbies, or spending time with loved ones. Self-care can also include taking care of physical and emotional needs, such as eating well, getting enough sleep, and practicing relaxation techniques.

Forgiveness is another important aspect of healing from narcissistic abuse. This does not mean excusing or minimizing the abuser's behavior but rather letting go of anger, bitterness, and resentment. Forgiveness can be a challenging and ongoing process, but it can also bring peace and freedom.

It is also important to work on rebuilding self-esteem and self-worth. Narcissistic abuse can leave individuals feeling worthless, helpless, and insecure. Through therapy, self-reflection, and positive self-talk, individuals can develop a more positive self-image and sense of self-worth.

Finally, moving forward from narcissistic abuse may involve creating a new life and identity. This can include setting new goals, pursuing new interests, and establishing new relationships. It may also include letting go of old beliefs and behavior patterns shaped by the abuse.

Healing from narcissistic abuse is a process that requires patience, self-compassion, and perseverance. It can be a difficult and emotional journey, but overcoming the effects of narcissistic abuse and creating a fulfilling and meaningful life is possible. With the proper support and resources, individuals can learn to trust again, rebuild their self-esteem, and find happiness and joy in their lives.

Narcissism can be detrimental to people in a relationship with a narcissist. It is, therefore, essential to recognize the warning signs of narcissism to protect oneself from potentially harmful relationships.

Narcissists overstate their achievements, lack empathy, and manipulate others to get what they want. They may also have an entitled attitude and struggle to take accountability for their actions. Understanding these signs can help individuals make informed decisions about their relationships.

Narcissists are known for their manipulative tactics and ability to control those around them. In this book, we will explore the strategies narcissists use to gain power and control over others. By understanding the narcissist playbook, individuals can protect themselves and learn to recognize these relationship tactics.

Chapter Eleven

Eight Common Traits Of A Narcissist:

Narcissists are some of the most challenging personalities to navigate, both in personal and professional settings. They can be charming, charismatic, and successful on the surface, but beneath their confident exterior lies a web of manipulations, insecurities, and toxic behavior.

There are many different types of narcissists, each with their own unique traits and tendencies. However, there are some common patterns of behavior that I experienced in my x-husband's narcissistic behavior. By understanding these traits and how they manifest in different contexts, readers will be better equipped to identify and deal with narcissistic individuals in their own lives. Whether you're trying to navigate a difficult family member, coworker, or romantic partner, this book will provide you with the tools and insights you need to protect yourself and thrive.

Grandiose sense of self-importance: Narcissists believe they are superior to others and often exaggerate their achievements and talents.

Preoccupation with fantasies of unlimited success, power, brilliance, beauty, or ideal love: Narcissists often have grandiose dreams of success, power, and fame and may pursue these goals at all costs.

Excessive need for admiration: Narcissists crave attention and respect from others and may go to great lengths to be noticed and praised.

Sense of entitlement: Narcissists believe they are entitled to special treatment and privileges and may act entitled and demanding.

Lack of empathy: Narcissists have little regard for the feelings or needs of others and may be insensitive to their pain or suffering.

Exploitative behavior: Narcissists may take advantage of others to achieve their goals and use people for their gain without regard for their well-being.

Envy and jealousy: Narcissists may be jealous of others they perceive as more successful or attractive than themselves and may become hostile or resentful towards them.

Arrogance and haughtiness: Narcissists may be condescending and dismissive towards others and believe they are always right.

Chapter Twelve

Six Signs That You Are In A Relationship With A Narcissist

Being in a relationship with a narcissist can be one of the most difficult and painful experiences a person can go through. Narcissists have a way of making their partners feel simultaneously adored and neglected, cherished and discarded. They are masters of manipulation and emotional abuse, using their charm and charisma to control and dominate those around them.

One of the biggest challenges of being in a relationship with a narcissist is simply identifying the problem. Narcissists are skilled at hiding their true selves, and often their partners don't realize what's happening until they're deeply entangled in the relationship. Here are six signs that you are in a relationship with a narcissist.

Gaslighting

Narcissism and gaslighting are closely linked behaviors that can cause significant harm to those around them. Gaslighting is a tactic used by narcissists to manipulate others into questioning their perception of reality. At the same time, narcissism is a personality disorder characterized by a grandiose sense of self-importance, a lack of empathy, and a constant need for attention and admiration.

Narcissists often use gaslighting to control those around them. They may deny facts or manipulate the truth to make the other person doubt their own memory or perception. By making the other person feel crazy or unstable, the narcissist gains power and control in the relationship. Gaslighting can lead to feelings of confusion, self-doubt, and even trauma for those who experience it.

Narcissists may also use gaslighting to avoid taking responsibility for their actions. They may blame others for their mistakes or project their flaws onto others, leaving the other person feeling confused and unsure of themselves. This form of emotional abuse can be challenging to detect, as the narcissist may seem charming and charismatic on the surface.

Gaslighting can have severe consequences for those who experience it. It can lead to feelings of anxiety, depression, and even post-traumatic stress disorder (PTSD). Victims of gaslighting may feel like they are going crazy or losing touch with reality. Seeking support from loved ones and professionals is essential if you suspect you are being gaslit by a narcissist.

In conclusion, narcissism and gaslighting are toxic behaviors that can cause significant harm to those around them. Recognizing the signs of narcissistic behavior and seeking support if you are experiencing gaslighting or emotional abuse is essential. Remember, you deserve to be treated with respect and dignity in all your relationships.

Love Bombing

Narcissism and love bombing are two behaviors that are often seen in a romantic relationship with a narcissist. Love bombing is a tactic narcissists use to overwhelm their partner with affection and attention in the beginning stages of the relationship. This can be a form of manipulation that is used to control and exploit the other person.

Love bombing involves showering the other person with gifts, compliments, and attention. The narcissist may make grand gestures and profess their love and devotion intensely and overwhelmingly. This can make the other person feel unique and valued, but it can also be a way for the narcissist to gain control and manipulate the relationship.

Narcissists may use love bombing to lure their partner into a relationship and then use it to maintain control. Once the partner is hooked, the narcissist may exhibit more negative behaviors, such as devaluing, gaslighting, or even abuse. This can be confusing and traumatic for the other person, who may feel trapped in the relationship.

Love bombing can also be a way for a narcissist to boost their ego and sense of self-importance. They may enjoy the attention and admiration that they receive from their partner, but they may not be capable of reciprocating or maintaining a healthy relationship.

In conclusion, love bombing is a common tactic narcissists use to manipulate and control their partners in romantic relationships. It is important to be aware of the signs of love bombing and to seek support if you suspect that you are in a relationship with a narcissist. Remember, you deserve to be in a healthy and respectful relationship.

Projection

Narcissism is a personality disorder characterized by a sense of entitlement, a need for admiration, and a lack of empathy for others. People with narcissistic traits often engage in projection, a defense mechanism where they project their negative traits or feelings onto others. This can be a way for a narcissist to avoid taking responsibility for their own behavior and to maintain their sense of superiority.

Projection is a common tactic used by narcissists to manipulate and control others. For example, a narcissistic boss always late to meetings may accuse their employees of being disorganized or lazy. This can create confusion and self-doubt among the employees, who may begin to question their own competence.

Projection can also be a way for a narcissist to maintain their idealized self-image. They may project their flaws onto others to support the belief that they are perfect and infallible. This can be a way for a narcissist to protect their fragile ego and avoid feelings of shame or inadequacy.

In addition to projecting negative traits, narcissists may project their own positive qualities onto others. For example, narcissistic parent may see their child as an extension of themselves and project their talents or achievements onto the child. This can put a lot of pressure on the child to live up to the parent's expectations, leading to feelings of inadequacy or low self-esteem.

Projection can also be a form of gaslighting, where the narcissist manipulates the other person's perception of reality. By projecting their flaws onto others, the narcissist can make the other person doubt their judgment and feel like they are going crazy. This can be a very effective way for the narcissist to maintain control over the other person.

It is important to recognize projection as a tactic used by narcissists and to seek support if you suspect you are in a relationship with a narcissist. Remember that projection is a defense mechanism the narcissist uses to avoid taking responsibility for their behavior. It is not a reflection of your own worth or competence.

Narcissism and projection are two behaviors that often go hand in hand. Projection is a defense mechanism narcissists use to avoid taking responsibility for their behavior and maintain their sense of superiority. It can be a way for the narcissist to manipulate and control others, leading to confusion, self-doubt, and low self-esteem in the other person. If you suspect you are in a relationship with a narcissist, it is crucial to seek support and recognize that projection is not a reflection of your own worth or competence.

Narcissism And Triangulation

Narcissism and triangulation are two concepts that are closely related. Triangulation is a manipulative tactic that narcissists often use to create drama and conflict in their relationships. It involves bringing a third person into a relationship or situation, often to serve as a mediator or ally, and using this person to further their agenda.

Narcissists are known for their ability to charm and manipulate others, and they often use triangulation to keep people under their control. They may introduce a new person into a relationship, such as a coworker or a friend, and create a sense of competition between this person and their partner. This can lead to jealousy, conflict, and feelings of insecurity, all of which can make the narcissist feel more powerful and in control.

Triangulation can also be a way for the narcissist to create a sense of chaos and confusion, making it difficult for the other person to trust their judgment or intuition. For example, a narcissistic parent may pit one child against another, creating a sense of rivalry and tension between them. This can be a way for the parent to maintain control over the children and avoid being held accountable for their behavior.

Another way that narcissists use triangulation is by playing the victim and seeking sympathy from others. They may manipulate a friend or family member into believing that they are the victim of abuse or mistreatment when they are the ones causing the problems in the relationship. This action can be a way for the narcissist to gain sympathy and support while avoiding accountability for their conduct.

Triangulation can also be used to control the information that is shared between people. For example, a narcissistic boss may assign a project to two employees and give them conflicting instructions. This can create confusion and conflict between the employees, making it difficult for them to work together effectively. The boss can then step in and play the role of mediator, further strengthening their control over the situation.

It is vital to recognize triangulation as a manipulative tactic used by narcissists and to seek support if you are in a relationship with a narcissist. Remember that triangulation is a way for the narcissist to maintain control over the other person and does not reflect your worth or competence.

If you suspect that you are in a relationship with a narcissist who is using triangulation, there are several things you can do to protect yourself:

Try to maintain your sense of self-worth and self-esteem, and do not allow the narcissist to manipulate your emotions or feelings of self-worth.

Seek support from friends or family members who can provide a safe and supportive environment.

Consider seeking professional help from a therapist or counselor who can help you navigate the challenges of being in a relationship with a narcissist.

Narcissism And Discard

Discard is a term used in the context of narcissistic relationships. It refers to abruptly ending a relationship or connection with someone a narcissist previously idealized. This behavior is one of the hallmark traits of narcissistic personality disorder, and it can cause significant emotional damage to the person who is being discarded.

When a narcissist is in the idealization phase of a relationship, they make the other person feel incredibly special and valued. They may shower them with gifts, attention, and affection, leading the other person to believe that they have found their perfect partner. However, as the relationship progresses, the narcissist begins to devalue their partner, finding faults with them and criticizing them for things that they once found endearing.

Eventually, the narcissist will reach a point where they no longer feel any emotional attachment to their partner. At this stage, they may engage in discard behavior, abruptly ending the relationship without any explanation or warning. This can leave the other person feeling confused, hurt, and traumatized.

One of the reasons that narcissists engage in discard behavior is that they have an intense fear of intimacy and commitment. They may find it difficult to maintain emotional connections with others because they focus on their needs and desires. Discarding a partner allows them to avoid the discomfort of emotional intimacy and move on to someone new who they can idealize and devalue all over again.

Another reason that narcissists engage in discard behavior is that they are seeking validation and attention. They may enjoy the power and control that comes with abruptly ending a relationship, knowing that their partner will be left feeling devastated and desperate for closure.

Discard behavior is often a part of the narcissistic cycle of abuse, which includes idealization, devaluation, and discards. It is a way for narcissist to maintain their power and control over their partner, keeping them in constant emotional turmoil.

The aftermath of a discard can be complicated for the person left behind. They may struggle to understand why the relationship ended so suddenly and without warning, and they may feel as though they have been abandoned. They may also experience feelings of worthlessness, shame, and guilt, believing they are responsible for the breakup.

It is important for people who have experienced discard behavior to seek support and counseling to help them process their emotions and heal from the trauma. They may need to rebuild their self-esteem and learn to trust others again after being hurt by a narcissist.

Overall, discard behavior is a common tactic narcissists use to maintain power and control over their partners. It can be incredibly damaging to the person who is being dumped, causing emotional trauma and feelings of abandonment. It is important for individuals who have experienced this type of behavior to seek support and counseling to help them heal and move forward.

Chapter Thirteen

The Effects of Narcissism On Friendships And Relationships

My husband's narcissism didn't just affect our marriage - it had a profound impact on our friendships as well. In the early days of our relationship, we were both part of a close-knit group of friends. We spent countless weekends together, exploring the city, trying new restaurants, and enjoying each other's company.

But as our relationship progressed, my husband's true colors began to emerge. He became increasingly self-centered and demanding, always insisting on having his way and belittling those who didn't agree with him. He would interrupt conversations and talk over others, dominating the group dynamic with his grandiose stories and opinions.

At first, our friends tried to brush off my husband's behavior, chalking it up to his personality quirks. But over time, it became clear that his narcissism was taking a toll on everyone. People started to avoid spending time with us, or would make excuses when we invited them out. The once-vibrant group dynamic had devolved into a tense, uncomfortable atmosphere.

Looking back, I can see how my husband's narcissism slowly eroded our friendships. He was unable to see beyond his own needs and desires, and couldn't handle any challenge to his authority or status. He was quick to lash out at anyone who threatened his ego, creating a toxic and unsustainable environment.

It's been years since we've spoken to most of those friends, and while it's painful to think about what we've lost, I know that the blame lies squarely on my husband's shoulders. His narcissism destroyed our relationships with people we once cared about deeply, and it's a loss that still haunts me to this day.

Narcissistic behavior can have a significant impact on the people around the individual. Narcissists may struggle to form meaningful relationships and often prioritize their needs over others. They may also struggle with depression, anxiety, and addiction due to their self-centered tendencies. Moreover, the constant need for validation and admiration can lead to an unhealthy cycle of dependence on external sources of validation.

Narcissism can have significant negative effects on friendships and relationships. Here are some ways in which narcissism can impact these connections:

Lack of empathy: Narcissists often have difficulty understanding and empathizing with the feelings of others. This can lead to a lack of emotional support and validation in friendships and relationships.

Exploitative behavior: Narcissists may use others for their gain without regard for their well-being. This misuse can lead to feelings of betrayal and mistrust in friendships and relationships.

Arrogance and entitlement: Narcissists may believe they are entitled to special treatment and privileges and may become angry or resentful when they don't receive them. This resentment can lead to conflicts and tension in friendships and relationships.

A constant need for admiration: Narcissists often crave attention and validation from others and may become upset or angry when they don't receive it. This need can lead to exhaustion and frustration in friendships and relationships.

Lack of reciprocity: Narcissists may have difficulty giving back to others and may not prioritize the needs of their friends or partners. This behavior can lead to neglect and resentment in friendships and relationships.

Jealousy and envy: Narcissists may become jealous of their friends or partners, especially if they perceive them as more successful or attractive. This jealousy can lead to feelings of competition and resentment in friendships and relationships.

Narcissism can make it difficult to form and maintain healthy friendships and relationships. It's important to recognize the signs of narcissism and to set boundaries to protect yourself and your emotional well-being.

Coping with Narcissism In A Friendship or Relationship

Coping with narcissistic behavior can be challenging, but there are several strategies individuals can use to protect themselves. Setting boundaries, practicing self-care, and seeking support from loved ones can help individuals maintain healthy relationships. It is also essential to seek professional help to address the underlying causes of selfish behavior and develop healthy coping mechanisms.

Being in a relationship with a narcissistic partner can be very challenging and emotionally exhausting. Narcissists often have an inflated sense of self-importance and can be extremely self-centered, lacking empathy and consideration for others. However, there are several coping strategies you can use to deal with a narcissistic partner:

Set boundaries: It is vital to set clear boundaries with your partner and communicate your expectations. Let them know what you are willing to tolerate and what you will not accept.

Avoid engaging in arguments: Narcissists can be very argumentative and often engage in verbal attacks. Avoid engaging in discussions as it only fuels their ego and gives them the attention they crave.

Focus on self-care: Narcissists can drain your energy and emotional resources. Take care of yourself by engaging in activities that make you feel good, such as exercise, meditation, or spending time with loved ones.

Seek support: It can be helpful to seek help from friends, family, or a therapist who can provide you with a safe space to express your feelings and offer guidance.

Practice assertiveness: Narcissists can be very manipulative and controlling. Practice being assertive and standing up for yourself without aggression or hostility.

Consider leaving the relationship: If the narcissism is extreme and is causing you emotional or physical harm, consider leaving the relationship. It can be not easy, but sometimes it is the best decision for your well-being. Remember, coping with a narcissistic partner requires patience and persistence. By setting boundaries, taking care of yourself, and seeking support, you can navigate the relationship and protect your emotional well-being.

Outmaneuvering A Narcissist And Maintaining Your Self Worth

Outsmarting narcissists can be challenging, as they tend to be skilled at manipulation and have a strong desire for control. However, there are a few strategies that may help in dealing with a narcissist.

One of the most important things to remember is to set boundaries. Narcissists often lack empathy and are known for pushing boundaries. It is vital to establish clear limits and stick to them. This boundary can include limiting your time with them, what topics are off-limits, and what behaviors are unacceptable.

Another strategy is to practice detachment. Narcissists thrive on attention and may use emotional manipulation to try and keep you engaged. You can avoid getting caught up in their drama and manipulation by practicing emotional detachment.

Recognizing when the narcissist is attempting to gaslight you is also important. Gaslighting is a tactic narcissists use to make you question your perception of reality. You can avoid falling into this trap by keeping a journal or seeking the opinions of trusted friends or family members.

It is also important to maintain your sense of self-worth. Narcissists often try to tear down the self-esteem of those around them to maintain their sense of superiority. You can resist their attempts to tear you down by recognizing your strengths and focusing on positive self-talk.

Additionally, it can be helpful to seek support from others. Whether it is a therapist or a support group, having a community of people who understand what you are going through can be invaluable. They can provide validation, guidance, and a sense of belonging.

Another essential strategy is to avoid engaging in power struggles. Narcissists often see everything as a competition and may become combative if they feel you have threatened their control. You can avoid getting drawn into their game by avoiding these types of conflicts and staying calm.

Finally, it is essential to recognize when it is time to walk away. Sometimes, dealing with a narcissist may be too much to handle. If the relationship becomes too toxic or dangerous, cutting ties and moving on may be necessary. Outwitting a narcissist requires setting boundaries, emotional detachment, recognizing gaslighting, maintaining self-worth, seeking support, avoiding power struggles, and knowing when to walk away. While challenging, these strategies can help you navigate a relationship with a narcissist and protect yourself from their manipulation and control.

Narcissists Can Find Help: Treatment Options for Narcissism

Narcissistic Personality Disorder (NPD) is a challenging condition to treat. Treatment is usually sought when the disorder significantly affects the individual's life and relationships. Treatment options for narcissism include therapy, medication, and support groups. Here are some of the most common treatment options for narcissism:

Psychotherapy: Psychotherapy is the most common treatment for NPD. Cognitive-behavioral therapy (CBT) and psychodynamic therapy help individuals with NPD understand their thoughts, feelings, and behaviors. The goal of psychotherapy is to help the individual develop empathy and compassion for others and learn new ways of coping with negative emotions.

Medication: While no specific medicines for NPD exist, medication can help alleviate symptoms associated with co-occurring disorders such as depression or anxiety. Antidepressants, mood stabilizers, and anti-anxiety medications are often prescribed to individuals with NPD.

Group Therapy: Group therapy can be helpful for individuals with NPD to learn new social skills and develop better relationships with others. Support groups such as Narcissistic Anonymous can be beneficial for individuals with NPD to connect with others who have similar experiences.

Family Therapy: Family therapy can be helpful for individuals with NPD who have strained relationships with family members. Family therapy can help family members learn how to communicate effectively and understand each other's needs.

Dialectical Behavior Therapy (DBT): DBT is a form of therapy that combines elements of CBT and mindfulness-based therapy. DBT can be helpful for individuals with NPD to learn new coping skills, emotion regulation, and stress management techniques.

Self-Help Books and Workbooks: Many self-help books and workbooks are available for individuals with NPD. These resources can help provide individuals with NPD with a better understanding of their condition and to learn new coping skills.

Mindfulness Meditation: Mindfulness meditation can help individuals with NPD learn to manage their thoughts and emotions more effectively. Mindfulness meditation can help individuals with NPD develop greater self-awareness and improve their ability to regulate emotions.

Hypnotherapy: Hypnotherapy can be helpful for individuals with NPD to access more profound levels of consciousness and gain greater insight into their condition. Hypnotherapy can help individuals with NPD to understand the underlying reasons for their behavior and to learn new coping skills.

Art Therapy: Art therapy can be helpful for individuals with NPD to express their emotions and gain greater self-awareness. Art therapy can help individuals with NPD to develop greater empathy and compassion for others.

Lifestyle Changes: Individuals with NPD may benefit from lifestyle changes such as reducing stress, improving sleep habits, and engaging in regular exercise. These changes can help individuals with NPD improve their overall mental health and well-being.

Treating NPD can be challenging, but with therapies, medication, and lifestyle changes, individuals with NPD can learn to manage their symptoms and improve their overall quality of life. It is essential to seek treatment from a qualified mental health professional who specializes in treating NPD to receive the best possible care.

Narcissism is a complex personality disorder that can have far-reaching effects on individuals and their loved ones. Recognizing the signs of narcissism and seeking professional help to address the underlying causes is essential. With the proper support and treatment, individuals can overcome narcissistic tendencies and develop healthy relationships based on mutual respect and empathy.

Chapter Fourteen

Leaving A Narcissist

As I sit here reflecting on my life, I can't help but wish I had left my narcissistic husband earlier. I spent years trying to make things work, believing that if I just loved him enough or tried hard enough, he would change. But in reality, I was only delaying the inevitable.

My husband's narcissism had become a toxic presence in our relationship, leaving me feeling isolated, unappreciated, and emotionally drained. He was never satisfied with anything I did, constantly demanding more and more from me while refusing to acknowledge my needs or feelings.

Despite all of this, I stayed with him. I was convinced that I could make things work, that I could somehow fix him or save our relationship. But in reality, I was only hurting myself. By staying with a narcissist, I was allowing myself to be slowly chipped away, my self-esteem and sense of self-worth eroded over time.

Looking back, I know that leaving my husband was the best thing I could have done for myself. It wasn't easy, and there were certainly times when I second-guessed my decision. But ultimately, I knew that I deserved better than what he was able to give me. I deserved a partner who would love and support me, not someone who would use me as a pawn in their own personal game.

If you're reading this and find yourself in a similar situation, I urge you to trust your instincts. Don't wait as long as I did to take action. You deserve to be treated with love, respect, and kindness, and if your partner isn't able to provide those things, then it may be time to move on.

Leaving a narcissist can be challenging and complex, but it is essential for your mental and emotional well-being. Here are some steps you can take to leave a narcissist:

Recognize the signs of narcissistic behavior: Remember, narcissists tend to have an inflated sense of self-importance, lack empathy, and have an excessive need for admiration. Understanding these traits can help you recognize if you are dealing with a narcissist.

Create a support system: Leaving a narcissist can be difficult, and it is vital to have a support system of friends and family who can help you through the process.

Make a plan: Before leaving, create a plan of action. This plan may involve finding a safe place to stay, saving money, and making arrangements for children or pets.

Set boundaries : Narcissists often push boundaries and make it difficult for others to assert themselves. Setting clear boundaries and sticking to them can help you regain control and independence.

Seek professional help: It can be helpful to speak with a therapist or counselor who has experience working with individuals who have experienced narcissistic abuse. They can provide the support and guidance you need to leave safely.

Remember that leaving a narcissist is a process that takes time and patience. But by taking these steps, you can regain control of your life and move forward in a healthier and more positive direction.

Getting Over A Narcissist And reclaiming Your Happiness

Getting over a narcissist you love can be difficult and painful, but it is possible. Here are some steps you can take:

R ecognize the narcissist's behavior:
Understand that the narcissist's behavior is not your fault and that you cannot change them. They may have manipulated, belittled, and made you feel like you are not good enough. Recognize that their behavior reflects their issues, not yours.

Allow yourself to grieve: Feeling sad, angry, and hurt after a relationship with a narcissist is okay. Allow yourself to mourn the loss of the relationship and the person you thought they were.

Cut off contact: Moving on from the abuse will be difficult, and it may be necessary to cut off contact with the narcissist. This ordeal can be harrowing, especially if you have strong feelings for them, but it is essential to remember that staying in touch will only prolong the pain.

Focus on self-care: Take care of yourself physically, emotionally, and mentally. Exercise, eat well, and get enough sleep. Engage in activities that make you happy, such as hobbies or spending time with friends and family.

Seek support: Surround yourself with people who love and support you. Consider speaking with a therapist or counselor who can provide you with guidance and support as you work through your feelings.

Practice self-compassion: Be kind to yourself and give yourself time to heal. Remember that recovering from a relationship with a narcissist takes time and effort, but it is possible to move on and find happiness again.

Remember , you deserve to be treated with love and respect, and you have the power to create a better future for yourself.

Chapter Fifteen

The Future of Narcissism: Trends and Implications.

Narcissism has been a topic of study and fascination for decades, and as our understanding of this complex personality disorder continues to evolve, so too does our perception of its future. With the rise of social media and a culture that often prioritizes self-promotion and individualism over communal values, many experts believe that narcissism is becoming more prevalent in society. But what will the future hold for this personality disorder, and how will it impact the way we relate to one another? Will we see a shift towards empathy and community-mindedness, or will the cult of the individual continue to reign supreme? Only time will tell, but as our understanding of narcissism deepens, we may be better equipped to navigate the challenges that lie ahead.

The future of narcissism is a topic of great interest and concern, as the prevalence of narcissistic traits and behaviors seems to be on the rise in recent years. Here are ten trends and implications to consider:

Social media: The increasing use of social media has been linked to the rise of narcissistic tendencies, allowing individuals to present a curated and idealized version of themselves to the world.

Technology: Advances in technology, such as virtual reality and artificial intelligence, may provide new avenues for narcissistic expression and self-promotion.

Cultural shifts: Changes in cultural norms, such as focusing on individualism and self-expression, may contribute to the increasing prevalence of narcissistic traits.

Mental health: Narcissistic personality disorder (NPD) is a recognized mental health disorder, and it is likely that more research will be conducted on the causes and treatment of this condition in the future.

Relationships: The impact of narcissism on relationships is of great interest, and there may be a greater focus on developing strategies for coping with narcissistic individuals in the future.

Parenting: Parenting styles and practices may also come under scrutiny concerning the development of narcissistic traits in children and adolescents.

Education: Educators and researchers may seek to develop interventions and educational programs to reduce the prevalence of narcissistic traits and promote empathy and compassion.

Politics: The rise of populist and authoritarian leaders have been linked to narcissistic traits, and the impact of narcissism on politics may be a growing concern.

Workplace: The impact of narcissistic behavior in the workplace may continue to be a focus of research and intervention, with a greater emphasis on creating healthy work environments.

Prevention: While there is no known cure for narcissistic personality disorder, prevention efforts may focus on identifying and addressing early signs of narcissistic behavior in individuals, such as entitlement and lack of empathy.

Overall, the future of narcissism is complex and multifaceted, with implications for mental health, relationships, politics, and society as a whole. It is vital for researchers, practitioners, and individuals to remain vigilant and informed about the potential impact of narcissistic behavior and to work towards creating healthier and more empathic communities.

If you are in a relationship with someone narcissistic and abusive, you can find help by dialing the number for NATIONAL DOMESTIC HOTLINE @800-799-7233

Made in the USA
Columbia, SC
07 December 2024

48673644R00062